Memoir in the Margins of Psalms

Journaling Your Story in the Margins of God's Story

ROBIN GRUNDER

Published by Legacy Press Books, an imprint of End Game Press
LegacyPressBooks.org
Your life tells a story; we can help you write it.

For permission, please write to **robin@robingrunder.org**

Printed in the United States of America

ISBN: 978-1-63797-153-6

Edited by Twila Belk

Cover and interior design and layout by Nelly Murariu @PixBeeDesign.com

Dedication

I dedicate this book to my husband, Brian, who has dedicated his life to supporting me.

Introduction

Has anything like this ever happened in your days
or in the days of your ancestors?
Tell it to your children,
and let your children tell it to their children,
and their children to the next generation.

Joel 1:2–3 (NIV)

I've been helping people compile, record, and write their life stories and memoirs for almost twenty years. Sometimes the stories are professionally published or bound, sometimes they are kept in handwritten journals, and sometimes they are digitally published. No matter how each story is preserved, they all share the same purpose—to create a connection with future family generations by telling the stories that shaped the person who wrote them.

A few years back, my husband signed up with a genealogy researching site and became fascinated with tracing his family tree back as far as he could. Recording names and dates he found prompted him to call his parents and ask what they knew about some of the family members.

My in laws pulled out a box of old photos, scrapbooks, newspaper clippings, and other documents that had been collected from his grandparents and great-grandparents. Among those items were two Bibles. One was presented to my husband's great-grandmother in 1888; the other was a pocket-sized New Testament presented to his great-grandfather in 1903.

As we thumbed through the brittle, yellowed pages, we stopped at all the places where a verse was underlined, a note was penned in the margin, and a date or name was written. Those markings caused us both to pause, read the related Scripture, and wonder what my husband's great-grandparents might have been thinking, praying, or experiencing at the time they read the passage. We could almost feel them interacting with the verses and clinging to the words on the page. It became clear to us that the Bibles were never far from my husband's great-grandparents.

Even though we had never met them, we felt connected to his ancestors. And because we could see how they interacted with the words in the Scriptures, we felt a closer connection to God.

In the margins of those Bibles, my husband's great-grandparents did the same thing I help my clients do—they left a written legacy through penned prayers, underlined words, and special notes.

I'm sure they never expected their Bibles to be passed down to generations they'd never meet. Nor would they have expected anyone other than themselves to be interested in looking back on the notes they made. But their own thoughts in their own handwriting in the margins of their own Bibles have helped my husband and me to know more about them than just the information on a genealogy report. It has helped us understand who they were and what was important to them at a certain time in our family's history.

Memoir in the Margins of Psalms is meant for you to do the same—create a connection between your story and God's Word, and to connect future generations to both. It's a way to leave a written legacy of how you want to be known and remembered directly on the pages of how God wants to be known and remembered.

This journal can be used in a couple of different ways. First, you can do exactly what the journal is designed for and read the Scripture and answer the journaling prompts right on these pages. Another way you can use this journal is to use the prompts and write your answers directly on the pages of your own journaling Bible, turning your Bible into a written legacy or gift for your family members.

The prompts are short and simple to not overwhelm you into thinking you must write an essay response to each one. Some will ask you to record different factual details about your life, some will focus on memories, and others will help draw out the stories you are currently living.

If you are interested in Bible journaling, you can also add artwork and photographs either to this journal or in your own Bible. This brings a visual element to your life story.

Why is this important?

Someday your children, grandchildren, and the children of your grandchildren will want to know about you. Why? Because they came from you. Understanding more about you, your life experiences, and how you viewed the world will help them know more about themselves.

The Bible is full of commands to remember and pass on the stories of the past so that people would know how to live in the present and leave a legacy for the future. When God's people remembered the stories and understood who they were, they prospered. When the stories stopped, they wandered into disaster, no longer understanding who they were.

As in biblical times, our stories are never more than one generation from being lost.

My prayer for you as you use and personalize this journal or your own Bible is that you will see how God has been at work in your life and pass your story, your wisdom, and your life experiences on to your family members.

Robin Grunder

Lead me in the right path, O Lord,
or my enemies will conquer me.
Make your way plain for me to follow.

Psalm 5:8 (NLT)

In which areas of your life are you seeking direction right now?

I am worn out from sobbing.
All night I flood my bed with weeping,
drenching it with my tears.

Psalm 6:6 (NLT)

Do you currently or have you ever suffered from depression? Tell about your experience. What have you found to be helpful when despair hits?

Lord my God, I take refuge in you;
save and deliver me from all who pursue me.
Psalm 7:1 (NIV)

God is stronger than any adversity we could ever face. What situations are you facing that you need God's strength to get through?

When I consider your heavens,
the work of your fingers,
the moon and the stars
which you have set in place,
what is mankind that you are mindful of them,
human beings that you care for them?

Psalm 8:3–4 (NIV)

The same God who created the sun, moon, and stars created and cares for you. Do you believe this? Write your own psalm of praise using Psalm 8 as a guide.

I will praise you, Lord,
with all my heart;
I will tell of all the marvelous things
you have done.

Psalm 9:1 (NLT)

What marvelous things has God done in your life? Write about them and why you never want to forget them.

Why do the wicked get away with despising God?
They think, "God will never call us to account."

Psalm 10:13 (NLT)

When you look at things going on in the world today, does it seem as if wicked people and evil situations are succeeding without remorse or consequence? List some of the things you've noticed and then remind yourself that God sees, he is just, and he will protect and preserve his people.

For the righteous Lord loves justice.
The virtuous will see his face.
Psalm 11:7 (NLT)

Do you ever feel unsafe when speaking the truth for fear that those who oppose God and his ways will attack you? Tell about it.

Help, O Lord, for the godly are fast disappearing!
The faithful have vanished from the earth!

Psalm 12:1 (NLT)

Write a prayer for your loved ones—that they do not become a part of the "disappearing faithful."

Lord, rise up and protect my loved ones from a culture of ego, self-sufficiency, and a breakdown of moral standards.

How long must I wrestle with my thoughts and day after day have sorrow in my heart?

Psalm 13:2 (NIV)

What sorrowful inner thoughts have you struggled with? Pray with confidence that God hears you and ask for comfort in the midst of your pain.

**The fool says in his heart,
"There is no God."**

Psalm 14:1 (NIV)

How do you respond to a person who holds different religious views than you?

Lord, who can dwell in your tent?
Who can live on your holy mountain?
Psalm 15:1 (CSB)

Jesus's death and resurrection is your invitation to dwell with him forever. Do you ever feel unworthy to enter God's presence? What makes you feel that way?

You direct me on the path
that leads to a beautiful life.
As I walk with You, the pleasures
are never-ending,
and I know true joy and contentment.

Psalm 16:11 (VOICE)

Are you currently experiencing true joy and contentment? If you are, share about it. If not, ask God to direct you to the path that leads to a beautiful life and abundant joy.

O Lord, hear my plea for justice.
Listen to my cry for help.
Pay attention to my prayer,
for it comes from honest lips.

Psalm 17:1 (NLT)

Write a prayer of protection for your family.

I called to the Lord, who is worthy of praise,
and I was saved from my enemies.

Psalm 18:3 (CSB)

Recall a time when God rescued you from hardship. Praise him for hearing your voice.

The heavens declare the glory of God;
the skies proclaim the work of his hands.

Psalm 19:1 (NIV)

How does God reveal himself through creation to you?

God, when I see the colors of the sunrise or sunset, I'm in awe that you set the sun in place for me. When I gaze at the night sky glittering with stars, I'm amazed that you placed each one. Looking at your heavens makes me want to praise you, just as your creation declares your glory.

May he grant your heart's desires
and make all your plans succeed.

Psalm 20:4 (NLT)

What are your heart's desires? Your hopes and dreams? List some of them here and ask God to show you whether they align with his purpose and plans for success in your life.

Through the victories you gave, his glory is great;
you have bestowed on him splendor and majesty.

Psalm 21:5 (NIV)

What is the biggest obstacle you have overcome?

**My God, my God, why have you forsaken me?
Why are you so far from saving me,
so far from my cries of anguish?**

Psalm 22:1 (NIV)

Write about a time when you felt hopeless or that God was far from you.

God, I've had the helpless feeling that David expresses in this Psalm. But I know you are near, even when I can't "feel" it. When everything seems to go against me, show me that you are near to my broken heart.

The Lord is my shepherd; I shall not want.
He makes me lie down in green pastures.
He leads me beside still waters.
He restores my soul.
He leads me in paths of righteousness for his name's sake.
Even though I walk through the valley of the shadow of death,
I will fear no evil, for you are with me;
your rod and your staff, they comfort me.
You prepare a table before me in the presence of my enemies;
you anoint my head with oil;
my cup overflows.
Surely goodness and mercy shall follow me all the days of my life,
and I shall dwell in the house of the Lord forever.

Psalm 23 (ESV)

Psalm 23 is probably the most familiar Psalm in the Bible. Read through it and jot down what stands out to you today.

The earth is the Lord's,
and everything in it,
the world, and all who live in it.

Psalm 24:1 (NIV)

God made the sky, the birds, and the trees, and he made you—all for his glory. Where do you see God's glory in you or around you?

Show me your ways, Lord,
teach me your paths.
Guide me in your truth and teach me,
for you are God my Savior,
and my hope is in you all day long.
Psalm 25:4–5 (NIV)

Write about a time you wandered off the path that God had for you.

Lord, I know I am prone to wander—not just in my actions, but in my thoughts and perspectives as well. Help me to daily check my actions and thoughts so that I am following where you guide.

Test me, Lord, and try me,
examine my heart and my mind.
Psalm 26:2 (NIV)

What areas in your life need refining?

The Lord is my light and my salvation—
whom shall I fear?
The Lord is the stronghold of my life—
of whom shall I be afraid?

Psalm 27:1 (NIV)

What are you most afraid of? Do you think it is wrong or unspiritual to feel afraid?

Listen to my prayer for mercy
as I cry out to you for help,
as I lift my hands toward your holy sanctuary.
Psalm 28:2 (NLT)

When you cry out to God for help, do you trust he is listening? Why or why not?

The Lord gives his people strength.
The Lord blesses them with peace.

Psalm 29:11 (NLT)

Finish this sentence: Lord, give me strength and peace about . . .

Weeping may last through the night,
but joy comes with the morning.
Psalm 30:5 (NLT)

What trial have you faced when it seemed as if there was no hope?

I had a relationship that I begged God for years to heal. This person, for good or for bad, was a part of my life to stay. Unfortunately, they were very hurtful toward me. I had come to terms with the idea that this person may never accept me or respond in a loving manner toward me, and my emotions about the entire situation were low.
But God . . .
He lifted me out of my sadness, a sadness I thought I would have to live with forever. And out of nowhere, and with nothing to do with my own efforts, God healed the relationship I had prayed about for many long nights.
One morning, joy truly came.

Love the Lord, all you godly ones!
For the Lord protects those who are loyal to him.

Psalm 31:23 (NLT)

Write a prayer that your children, grandchildren, and all those in future generations will be loyal, strong, and courageous, and place their loyalty in the Lord.

Finally, I confessed all my sins to you
and stopped trying to hide my guilt.
I said to myself, "I will confess my rebellion to the Lord."
And you forgave me! All my guilt is gone.

Psalm 32:5 (NLT)

Secret sins are usually accompanied by guilt and shame. Acknowledge any secret sins in your life and know that the God you serve is just and able and will forgive you.

May your faithful love rest on us, Lord,
for we put our hope in you.

Psalm 33:22 (CSB)

Sometimes the best way to remind ourselves that God is our protector, provider, and hope today is to reflect on his protection and provision in the past. List ways you've seen God's protection and provision throughout your life.

I will praise the Lord at all times.
I will constantly speak his praises.

Psalm 34:1 (NLT)

Thankfulness isn't just for Thanksgiving. Take time to list things you are grateful for and praise God for them here and throughout your day.

Don't let my treacherous enemies rejoice
over my defeat.
Don't let those who hate me without cause
gloat over my sorrow.

Psalm 35:19 (NLT)

Write about a time when following God caused others to attack you. Has God vindicated you in this particular battle?

How precious is your unfailing love, O God!
All humanity finds shelter
in the shadow of your wings.

Psalm 36:7 (NLT)

Do you feel secure in God's protection? Why or why not?

Trust in the Lord and do good.
Then you will live safely in the land and prosper.

Psalm 37:3 (NLT)

What good deeds do you like to do or have always wanted to do?

For I am waiting for you, O Lord.
You must answer for me, O Lord my God.

Psalm 38:15 (NLT)

Have you ever made a mistake that took a toll on you physically, emotionally, and socially? Tell about it and cry out to God to be near.

**"Lord, remind me how brief my time on earth will be.
Remind me that my days are numbered—
how fleeting my life is."**

How does this Psalm make you feel about the times you've procrastinated?

I waited patiently for the Lord,
and he turned to me and heard my cry for help.
Psalm 40:1 (CSB)

Write about a time when you waited patiently on God, and he answered your prayer in a way that went far above your expectations.

They visit me as if they were my friends,
but all the while they gather gossip,
and when they leave, they spread it everywhere.

Psalm 41:6 (NLT)

When have you trusted someone only to have that person turn on you?

Why am I discouraged?
Why is my heart so sad?
I will put my hope in God!
I will praise him again—
my savior and my God!

Psalm 42:5; Psalm 43:5 (NLT)

Pour out your real feelings to God here—on paper. He can handle it!

Psalm 43 is a continuation of Psalm 42. As you read them together, remember that when external circumstances cause internal despair, God is faithful, and you can express your feelings to him.

Rise up and help us;
redeem us because of your unfailing love.
Psalm 44:26 (NIV)

Finish this prayer:

Lord, every day I struggle with battles on the inside and on the outside. They are . . .

**I will cause your name to be remembered
for all generations;
therefore the peoples will praise you forever and ever.**

Psalm 45:17 (CSB)

What actions of yours will help those around you remember God's name?

Lord, help me live in a way that will point future generations of my family to you.

"Be still, and know that I am God."

Psalm 46:10 (NIV)

When life is crashing all around you, do you try harder to keep it all together? How does Psalm 46:10 inspire you to take a different approach?

Sing praises to God, sing praises;
sing praises to our King, sing praises!

Psalm 47:6 (NLT)

What is your favorite hymn or worship song? Write it out here.

Go, inspect the city of Jerusalem.
Walk around and count the many towers.
Take note of the fortified walls,
and tour all the citadels,
that you may describe them
to future generations.

Psalm 48:12–13 (NLT)

Take note of some of the beauty in your life and the beauty that surrounds you.

No one can redeem the life of another or give to God a ransom for them—

Psalm 49:7 (NIV)

Are you living for earthly wealth, fame, or recognition? None of that can save you or your loved ones when you pass away.

How can you place your focus on things eternal?

Lord, help me to not worry about money or find my happiness in things of this world.

**Make thankfulness your sacrifice to God,
and keep the vows you made to the Most High.**

Psalm 50:14 (NLT)

Respond to God with gratitude for who he is.

Don't keep looking at my sins.
Remove the stain of my guilt.
Psalm 51:9 (NLT)

Is there sin in your life you think God can't forgive? Guess what—he can! Confess your sin and ask God to restore the joy of salvation and forgiveness in your life.

**"Look what happens to mighty warriors
who do not trust in God.
They trust their wealth instead
and grow more and more bold in their wickedness."**

Psalm 52:7 (NLT)

When have you trusted in your own wealth, image, or works? How did that work out for you?

Oh, that salvation for Israel would come out of Zion!
When God restores his people,
let Jacob rejoice and Israel be glad!

Psalm 53:6 (NIV)

What are you believing God for today?

For you have rescued me from my troubles and helped me to triumph over my enemies.

Psalm 54:7 (NLT)

What troubles do you need to hand over to God today? Let him fight the battle for you.

Oh, that I had wings like a dove;
then I would fly away and rest.

Psalm 55:6 (NLT)

If you could escape to anywhere for rest, where would you go?

I am constantly hounded by those who slander me,
and many are boldly attacking me.

Psalm 56:2 (NLT)

Why can you still trust in God, even though he sometimes allows bad things to happen to you?

I cry out to God Most High,
to God, who vindicates me.

Psalm 57:2 (NIV)

Do you feel as if God has called you for a special purpose? What is it?

God, you are exalted above the heavens and the earth. I lift you up and give you the reigns of my life. Fulfill your purpose in me and remind me to turn to you as my strength.

Then people will say,
"Yes, there is a reward for the righteous!
There is a God who judges on earth!"

Psalm 58:11 (CSB)

What injustices burden your heart?

I will keep watch for you, my strength,
because God is my stronghold.

Psalm 59:9 (CSB)

In the middle of a chaotic time, how do you watch for signs that God is near?

With God we will gain the victory.

Psalm 60:12 (NIV)

What battle can you give to God and trust that he has already won?

Whether here on earth or when I'm in heaven, the ultimate victory is mine because God has already won—and I am his.

For you, God, have heard my vows;
you have given me the heritage of those who fear your name.

Psalm 61:5 (NIV)

Write a prayer for your family members—that they will find their refuge and strength in God alone and that they will be given the heritage of Christ.

O my people, trust in him at all times.
Pour out your heart to him,
for God is our refuge.

Psalm 62:8 (NLT)

Our world is constantly changing, but God remains the same. Pour out your heart to God—you can trust him.

I will be fully satisfied as with
the richest of foods;
with singing lips my mouth will praise you.

Psalm 63:5 (NIV)

What can you praise God for today?

They encourage each other to do evil
and plan how to set their traps in secret.
"Who will ever notice?" they ask.

Psalm 64:5 (NLT)

Evil exists all around us and it will be overcome. In the meantime, call on God to intervene where you see evil on the move.

For you answer our prayers.
All of us must come to you.
Psalm 65:2 (NLT)

God is faithful to hear our prayers. What are you praying for today?

Come and listen, all who fear God,
and I will tell what he has done for me.

Psalm 66:16 (CSB)

What are recent things you have seen God do in and around you?

May your ways be known throughout the earth,
your saving power among people everywhere.

Psalm 67:2 (NLT)

What is taking place on the global front? Write a prayer of blessing for the nations.

Praise be to the Lord, to God our Savior, who daily bears our burdens.

Psalm 68:19 (NIV)

Give your burdens over to God to carry.

Lord, just when I thought things were under control, our finances took a hard hit. I stand on your promise to bear my burden, and I rejoice today because I can trust you to provide for our needs.

Even my own brothers pretend they don't know me;
they treat me like a stranger.
Psalm 69:8 (NLT)

Have family members rejected you because of your faith?

Pray for them and for the next generation—that they will choose Christ as their salvation and that they, too, will inherit the kingdom of heaven.

But may all who search for you
be filled with joy and gladness in you.
May those who love your salvation
repeatedly shout, "God is great!"

Psalm 70:4 (NLT)

Pray for someone you know who seems to be searching for answers—that their search will lead to the joy and gladness found in God.

Even while I am old and gray,
God, do not abandon me,
while I proclaim your power
to another generation,
your strength to all who are to come.

Psalm 71:18 (CSB)

God's plan is bigger than just you and me. It's for entire generations. What message do you want to share with future generations of your family?

All kings will bow before him,
and all nations will serve him.

Psalm 72:11 (NLT)

Pray for the leaders of this country—that they would honor God in their lives and roles.

Lord, the world is home to a lot of unrest, fear, and oppression. I pray that our leaders will bow before you, that they will help those oppressed from violence, and that prosperity will come to our land.

**My health may fail, and my spirit may grow weak,
but God remains the strength of my heart;
he is mine forever.**

Psalm 73:26 (NLT)

Being blessed by God doesn't mean life is always easy. How can you relate to this Psalm?

**We no longer see your miraculous signs.
All the prophets are gone, and no one can
tell us when it will end.**

Psalm 74:9 (NLT)

In what ways have you seen a decline in morality and biblical beliefs in your lifetime? How does this prompt you to pray for your family and the next generation?

For God says, "I will break the strength of the wicked, but I will increase the power of the godly."

Psalm 75:10 (NLT)

God promises to bring justice against the wicked and increase the power of the godly. How does this bring you hope?

Make vows to the Lord your God,
and keep them.
Let everyone bring tribute to the
Awesome One.

Psalm 76:11 (NLT)

Psalm 76 lets us know we are on the winning side of the battle against evil. Acknowledge God for that today.

Your path led through the sea,
your way through the mighty waters,
though your footprints were not seen.

Psalm 77:19 (NIV)

What negative thoughts are you struggling with? Meditate on God's goodness, even if you can't see his footprints in your life right now.

I will open my mouth with a parable;
I will utter hidden things, things from of old—
things we have heard and known,
things our ancestors have told us.

Psalm 78:2–3 (NIV)

What stories have you heard about your ancestors that you want to tell the coming generation?

God, the nations have invaded your inheritance,
desecrated your holy temple,
and turned Jerusalem into ruins.

Psalm 79:1 (CSB)

Write a prayer for your nation based on the goodness of God.

Restore us, O God;
make your face shine on us,
that we may be saved.

Psalm 80:3 (NIV)

In what areas of your life or the world need healing and restoration?

**You shall have no foreign god among you;
you shall not worship any god other than me.**

Psalm 81:9 (NIV)

On what things, activities, or habits have you placed a higher value than God?

Rise up, God, judge the earth,
for all the nations belong to you.

Psalm 82:8 (CSB)

Have you ever gone on a short-term mission trip? Write a prayer for the children, the families, and others you met on the trip.

Let them know that you, whose name is the Lord—that you alone are the Most High over all the earth.

Psalm 83:18 (NIV)

What difficult people or circumstances can you give over to God today?

God, you are the Most High over everything and everyone. Remind me of this truth when I struggle with difficult people and circumstances.

Better is one day in your courts than a thousand elsewhere.

Psalm 84:10 (NIV)

How do you balance living in the moment and focusing on the future in a healthy way?

I listen carefully to what God the Lord is saying,
for he speaks peace to his faithful people.
But let them not return to their foolish ways.

Psalm 85:8 (NLT)

What habit do you tend to release to God only to repeatedly return to the same pattern?

Teach me your way, Lord,
that I may rely on your faithfulness;
give me an undivided heart,
that I may fear your name.

Psalm 86:11 (NIV)

Describe a time when you compromised to fit in with the world. Were you able to turn back to God with an undivided heart or do you still struggle with this situation?

When the Lord registers the nations, he will say, "They have all become citizens of Jerusalem."

Psalm 87:6 (NLT)

When you became a Christian, your name was recorded as a citizen of God's kingdom. What do you remember about that day?

May my prayer come before you;
turn your ear to my cry.

Psalm 88:2 (NIV)

What prayer requests do you have today? Bring them to God here.

I will sing about the Lord's faithful love forever;
I will proclaim your faithfulness to all generations
with my mouth.

Psalm 89:1 (CSB)

What story do you want to share with the future generations of your family?

Lord, I pray for all my children, grandchildren, and the generations that follow. If any of them are reading this, I pray they know and walk with you. Let them be filled with your love and joy and know that I have been praying for them before I ever knew their names.

A thousand years in your sight
are like a day that has just gone by.

Psalm 90:4 (NIV)

How can you adjust your schedule or mindset to make the most of each day?

For he will order his angels
to protect you wherever you go.
Psalm 91:11 (NLT)

When have you experienced what you believe was special protection from God's angels?

Even in old age they will still produce fruit;
they will remain vital and green.

Psalm 92:14 (NLT)

Those who are devoted to God will flourish, even in old age. How does this give you hope?

**But mightier than the violent raging of the seas,
mightier than the breakers on the shore—
the Lord above is mightier than these!**

Psalm 93:4 (NLT)

What storms are raging in your life right now? Do you believe that God is mightier than the storm?

When anxiety was great within me,
your consolation brought me joy.

Psalm 94:19 (NIV)

When we bring our private anxieties to God, he responds with consolation. Ask God to bring tender comfort to your soul today.

Today, if only you would hear his voice.

Psalm 95:7 (NIV)

God speaks to us even today. Soften your heart and listen. What is he saying to you?

Publish his glorious deeds among the nations.
Tell everyone about the amazing things he does.

Psalm 96:3 (NLT)

Describe an amazing way you've seen God intervene in your life or in someone close to you.

May all who are godly rejoice
in the Lord and praise his holy name!

Psalm 97:12 (NLT)

Pause and praise God for who he is.

Sing a new song to the Lord,
for he has performed wonders.

Psalm 98:1 (CSB)

What musical instruments have you learned to play or do you enjoy listening to?

Mighty King, lover of justice,
you have established fairness.
You have acted with justice
and righteousness throughout Israel.

Psalm 99:4 (NLT)

Do you see unfair things happening to you or around you? Ask God, the lover of justice, to establish fairness.

For the Lord is good,
and his faithful love endures forever;
his faithfulness, through all generations.

Psalm 100:5 (CSB)

Thank God for all he has done and will continue to do through you and your family.

I will be careful to lead a blameless life.

Psalm 101:2 (NIV)

Ask God to reveal any habits, thoughts, or actions that need to change. List them here.

Let this be recorded for future generations,
so that a people not yet born will praise the Lord.

Psalm 102:18 (NLT)

Take this opportunity to record a story from your childhood that you would like your family to know.

**Our days on earth are like grass;
like wildflowers, we bloom and die.**

Psalm 103:15 (NLT)

Is there a dream you have put off for a "better time?" What steps can you take today to move closer to that dream?

Lord, life is short. Help me to engage in conversations that will move me forward to whatever you have ordained for me.

How many are your works, Lord!
In wisdom you made them all;
the earth is full of your creatures.

Psalm 104:24 (NIV)

What aspect of nature speaks the most to you?

He always stands by his covenant—
the commitment he made to a thousand generations.

Psalm 105:8 (NLT)

God's promises to the descendants of Abraham, Isaac, and Jacob apply to you today. How does knowing this give you hope?

God, thank you that your promises are for me and will be for all generations that follow me. I pray that my kids, my grandchildren, and my great-grandchildren will know you, believe in your promises, and pass on a legacy of faith to their families.

They soon forgot his works
and would not wait for his counsel.

Psalm 106:13 (CSB)

What story from your life or from the Bible do you enjoy remembering? What does it teach you about God?

Let the redeemed of the Lord tell their story.

Psalm 107:2 (NIV)

How is life different for you with Jesus at the center?

**With God we will gain the victory,
and he will trample down our enemies.**

Psalm 108:13 (NIV)

What victory are you praying for today?

**For I am poor and needy,
and my heart is full of pain.**

Psalm 109:22 (NLT)

Describe a time when you were overcome with depression and pain.

God, I am overcome with depression right now. I ask, as the writer of Psalm 109:21 did, that you rescue me from this pain because you are faithful and good.

The Lord stands at your right hand to protect you.

Psalm 110:5 (NLT)

In what circumstances do you need to be reminded that God is with you?

He has caused his wonders to be remembered.

Psalm 111:4 (NIV)

Share a story of God's love in your life.

They do not fear bad news;
they confidently trust the Lord to care for them.

Psalm 112:7 (NLT)

How do these words comfort you when bad news threatens to shake your world?

He stoops to look down on heaven and on earth.

Psalm 113:6 (NLT)

God stoops down to lift us up. How has he lifted your outlook?

The Red Sea saw them coming and hurried out of their way!
The water of the Jordan River turned away.

Psalm 114:3 (NLT)

Describe a time when God seemed to open a door or create a path for you.

Not to us, Lord, not to us
but to your name be the glory,
because of your love and faithfulness.

Psalm 115:1 (NIV)

It's natural to want to be noticed or acknowledged for our accomplishments, sometimes forgetting that God created us for his glory. In what ways do you struggle with these mixed motives?

Because he bends down to listen,
I will pray as long as I have breath!

Psalm 116:2 (NLT)

God listens when you pray. What are you praying for today?

Praise the Lord, all you nations.
Praise him, all you people of the earth.
Psalm 117:1 (NLT)

Who are your local, regional, and national leaders right now? Write a prayer for them.

It is better to take refuge in the Lord than to trust in people.

Psalm 118:8 (NLT)

Would you describe yourself as a trusting person? Why or why not?

How can a young man stay on the path of purity?
By living according to your word.
Psalm 119:9 (NIV)

In what areas of your life do you have the most difficulty keeping purity in actions, thoughts, or motives?

I am tired of living
among people who hate peace.

Psalm 120:6 (NLT)

What people bring you the most peace when you are around them?

Lord, help me to dwell in literal and emotional places that bring your peace.

**I lift up my eyes to the mountains—
where does my help come from?
My help comes from the Lord,
the Maker of heaven and earth.**

Psalm 121:1–2 (NIV)

The maker of heaven and earth can help and protect you and your loved ones. What help and protection are you seeking today?

Pray for the well-being of Jerusalem:
"May those who love you be secure."
Psalm 122:6 (CSB)

What is currently going on in Israel? Write a prayer for the country's well-being.

I lift my eyes to you,
the one enthroned in heaven.

Psalm 123:1 (CSB)

Where do you look for comfort and security?

What if the Lord had not been on our side?

Psalm 124:1 (NLT)

How do you think your life would look if the Lord was not on your side?

As the mountains surround Jerusalem,
so the Lord surrounds his people
both now and forevermore.

Psalm 125:2 (NIV)

In a world filled with uncertainty, how does knowing that God surrounds you with his power and presence comfort you?

Those who plant in tears
will harvest with shouts of joy.

Psalm 126:5 (NLT)

What seeds are you sowing that have not yet produced a harvest? Pray with confidence and joy that you will see a harvest in this area.

Lord, I lift to you my child who does not fully embrace you. I pray that the seeds sown in their early life will bloom in the most beautiful way.

Unless the Lord builds the house,
the builders labor in vain.

Psalm 127:1 (NIV)

What goals or dreams would you like to achieve? Invite God to help you and to watch over those dreams.

Blessed are all who fear the Lord,
who walk in obedience to him.

Psalm 128:1 (NIV)

What causes you to doubt God when you are not successful in an endeavor?

But the Lord is good;
he has cut me free from the ropes of the ungodly.

Psalm 129:4 (NLT)

Have you ever been bullied as an adult? Share what happened.

From the depths of despair, O Lord,
I call for your help.
Psalm 130:1 (NLT)

What medical, physical, and spiritual components help you when you are feeling down?

**Instead, I have calmed and quieted myself,
like a weaned child who no longer cries for its
mother's milk.**

Psalm 131:2 (NLT)

When life seems to make no sense, how do you calm your mind and spirit?

For the Lord has chosen Jerusalem;
he has desired it for his home.

Psalm 132:13 (NLT)

What about your heavenly home are you most looking forward to?

How delightfully good
when brothers live together in harmony!
Psalm 133:1 (CSB)

Do you need to build a bridge with anyone? What steps can you take today to make your relationship more harmonious?

**Lift your hands toward the sanctuary,
and praise the Lord.**

Psalm 134:2 (NLT)

Praise God with open hands today. How is he speaking to you?

Your name, O Lord, endures forever;
your fame, O Lord, is known to every generation.

Psalm 135:13 (NLT)

God's legacy will last for all time. How are you making his name known in your time?

Lord, thank you for the positive influences I've had in my life. Help me to find ways for others to see you in me.

Give thanks to him who placed the earth among the waters.
His faithful love endures forever.

Psalm 136:6 (NLT)

The God who placed the earth and created the heavens is the same God who hears your prayers today. What would you like to thank him for?

"Sing us one of the songs of Zion."

Psalm 137:3 (CSB)

What was a favorite song from your youth? Why did you like it?

**The Lord will work out his plans for my life—
for your faithful love, O Lord, endures forever.**

Psalm 138:8 (NLT)

Has God surprised you with different plans for your life than what you had? In what way?

I praise you because I am fearfully and wonderfully made;
your works are wonderful,
I know that full well.

Psalm 139:14 (NIV)

Do you struggle with body image? Why is it hard to see yourself as God sees you—his beloved, priceless work of art?

Protect me, Lord,
from the power of the wicked.
Keep me safe from violent men
who plan to make me stumble.

Psalm 140:4 (CSB)

Ask God to provide a shield of protection from evil around you and your loved ones.

Let the godly strike me!
It will be a kindness!
If they correct me, it is soothing medicine.
Don't let me refuse it.

Psalm 141:5 (NLT)

Have you ever been called out in kindness on your words or actions? Was your heart open? What was the outcome?

When I am overwhelmed,
you alone know the way I should turn.
Psalm 142:3 (NLT)

When you are overwhelmed, where do you typically turn for comfort?

I remember the days of old.
I ponder all your great works
and think about what you have done.

Psalm 143:5 (NLT)

Recall a time when God came through for you. How can remembering this help you when you feel hopeless or afraid?

Reach down from heaven and rescue me.

Psalm 144:7 (NLT)

From what circumstances or battles do you need God to come to your rescue?

Let each generation tell its children of your mighty acts;
let them proclaim your power.

Psalm 145:4 (NLT)

Share a story of when God performed a mighty act in your life.

Do not put your trust in princes,
in human beings, who cannot save.

Psalm 146:3 (NIV)

When have you valued the opinion of others more than you should? What happened?

**He determines the number of stars
and calls them each by name.**

Psalm 147:4 (NIV)

How does knowing that the God of the universe loves you and calls you by name make you feel?

Lord, I love looking up at the stars in the night sky. I'm amazed that you placed each one and you even call them by name. It reminds me of how much you love and know me, placing me right where I am in this time in history.

Praise the Lord.
Praise the Lord from the heavens;
praise him in the heights above.

Psalm 148:1 (NIV)

What are some of the little things in life you enjoy?

Hallelujah!
Sing to the Lord a new song.
Psalm 149:1 (CSB)

What song would you like to sing to the Lord right now?

Let everything that has breath praise the Lord.
Praise the Lord.

Psalm 150:6 (NIV)

Write your own hymn of praise.

Made in the USA
Coppell, TX
03 March 2023